The centerpiece of *Odd Mercy* is "The Little Mommy Sonnets," a crown of sonnets that carries us poignantly through the life and death of the poet's mother, as well as their complicated bond over time. I was impressed with Gail Thomas' dedication to craft, her richness of detail and especially her deft transitions from the end line of one sonnet to the opening line of the next. The challenge here is to repeat the line, but to make it new, to show us another facet, and Thomas does that so skillfully in these poems, propelling us forward through the narrative. Poetry uses words to convey what is beyond words, to say the unsayable. The last line of *Odd Mercy* expresses this paradox tenderly as the poet reflects on her mother: "your words/now gibberish, your voice always in my head."

—Ellen Bass, Judge of the Charlotte Mew Prize

The stunning centerpiece of *Odd Mercy,* "The Little Mommy Sonnets" explores a complicated mother/daughter relationship that is turned on its head by dementia. "Did we find each other too late or just in time?" asks the daughter as her mother's "sharp tongue dissolves" and her own "armor melts." Beautifully written, heartfelt, generous, and forgiving, all the poems in this collection touched my heart deeply. Gail Thomas is a poet of tremendous talent.

—Lesléa Newman, author of *I Carry My Mother*

On *Waving Back* (2015)

These are poems of authority and grace, alive with the pulse of desire and the mystery of our deep connections.

—Joan Larkin

Thomas brings precise observation and earned wisdom to poems in which the "bitter and the sweet entwine."

—Robin Becker

Also by Gail Thomas

Waving Back (2015)

No Simple Wilderness: An Elegy for Swift River Valley (2001)

Finding the Bear (1997)

Odd Mercy

Winner of the Charlotte Mew Prize

Odd Mercy

Gail Thomas

Gail Thomas

For Faye —
With respect for your fine work.
Your Perugia sister —
Gail

Headmistress Press

ISBN-13:978-0997914924
ISBN-10:0997914920

Cover & book design by Mary Meriam.

P U B L I S H E R

Headmistress Press
60 Shipview Lane
Sequim, WA 98382
Telephone: 917-428-8312
Email: headmistresspress@gmail.com
Website: headmistresspress.blogspot.com

~ with deep respect for the families and caregivers
of people living with Alzheimer's and other
dementia-related illnesses

Contents

A Daughter's Garland

Mother
the dance reversed
spoon to mouth, shoes to feet
kisses allowed, even love words
who's there?

Mother
each day the same
in this place of hallways
kind strangers take my place, you say
thank you

Mother
we can rest now
with no expectations
the one you never knew is here
with you

Mother
I stroke your arm
play your favorite songs
your eyes are tidal, ebb and flow
hold on

Mother
an odd mercy
rains down on our grey heads
empty of memory and full
at once

Mother
an odd mercy
with no expectations
your eyes are tidal, ebb and flow
thank you

The Little Mommy Sonnets

"I will put Chaos into fourteen lines and keep him there..."

—*Edna St. Vincent Millay*

1

Your voice, always in my head until the shrinking,
until I could call you Little Mommy. When you lost
the family names, we watched them march out
the door holding hands with the hurts that kept us
licking our wounds. Now this mess of plaques
and tangles, a nest of lesser evils: to forget
the word for daughter or lose decades of strife.
Some people study for years at the feet of a master
to learn how to live in the moment. Your sharp
tongue dissolves to a soft fog, my armor melts,
the clear moment before us like a plowed field.
You fall asleep to the sound of my voice
humming something that makes you smile
before this long goodbye.

2

Before this long goodbye I move you closer,
winnow eighty years of living to two rooms.
Reduce the shirts, scarves and shoes you bought
again and again, the familiar color or cut, a balm.
Passenger now, you are awed by giant green
trees that hover over the road. You ask *why
are there so many and where do they come from?*
Like Vincent's pulsing cedars and lowering clouds,
these hills bear down. Stranger in a stranger land.
He, too, was the lone reaper just beyond hospital
walls who wrote *nature overpowers me.* You stare
out at the garden and fret about the mess
of feathers and shit that might keep wrens
from claiming their house in spring.

3

Each spring wrens claim their tiny house
on a pole next to the wood chopper whirligig
left behind by the old Russian who sold this plot.
Dirt is good, he said, and the roses go for broke.
The flannel shirted hewer hurls his axe and spins
in a furious show. I sip a margarita, watch a bird
swoop in and out with twiggy mouthfuls, chiding
and full of industry like you once were. Early
on Saturdays wielding broom and bucket you
bullied me out of bed. Dust was the enemy hiding
on sills and baseboards, ceiling and walls, waiting
for the swipe of your rag-wrapped mop. Beaten
carpets, polished floors, scrubbed porcelain – all
praised your worth, as I never did.

4

I never praised what you counted as worth,
the spotless rooms, well dressed children.
Armed with a toothbrush you visited me,
young mother fled to another state, husband
and house left behind. I bristled under
your attack on tub and toilet. If you had asked
what I needed, I couldn't have answered.
So like a heat-seeking missile you homed in:
divorce, second-floor apartment, mannish hair.
Your mother used to be so beautiful, you told
my daughters. How your own cheeks burned
imagining what your friends would say if they
knew about your good girl gone bad,
all that polish and shine wasted.

5

All that polish and shine wasted and daily pleas
to St. Jude, patron of lost causes, did not save
your girl. Three women in this apartment kitchen:
my lover and I stand hip to hip chopping onions
while you fume, *Whose kitchen is this?*
You've lost your place again. Like the time
your brothers went to school on the GI Bill
instead of you who won all A's. And your husband
with his university degree and pipe, dubbed
The Professor by your family, *so well-spoken.*
You sewed and cooked and cleaned till no one
could deny your gifts until this daughter who threw
it all away for this other one, stirring the pot.
You sit with empty hands and nothing smart to say.

6

With nothing smart to say, you always changed
the conversation from politics to a recipe.
Dad and I talked, you tuned out. Wars started
and ended, people marched in the streets, the word gay
was spoken on television, but you stayed out of it.
You went to Confession and Mass, counted
the collection basket for Father John, braided
a rug from old coats, sunbathed in the back yard.
I prodded. *Now's your chance to take classes.*
You refused, *It's too late.* Maybe the fog was
beginning its erasure and afraid of deep water,
you held fast to dry land. What did you see
in my eyes, this college smarty pants who
didn't want to shop like other daughters.

I did not want to shop like other daughters
or pray to plaster statues in the church that
shunned my father. He signed us over
when you married, sat alone at his church
every Sunday and holiday. Forbidden to go,
I imagined a brighter place where he would
sing in the choir, deliver meals to shut-ins,
a friendly minister would ask about us.
My brother and I fasted for the paper wafer,
mouthed empty words, watched a distant
priest flash the silver chalice, blood to wine.
You recited rote prayers, clicked a wooden
rosary to lessen your sentence in Purgatory,
lit a red votive for your own mother.

8

For remembrance, a red votive flickers but
you do not know who I am or that your good
man, my father, has died. It seemed kinder
not to shock you with the news once and then
again in an endless loop of sorrow. You don't
even ask where he is, so I do not explain how
I've been holding on to his absence for weeks.
Grieving him and grieving you not grieving him.
Where in your tangles is the letter you sent,
*the greatest sadness of my life is that you did
not baptize your girls.* I click on Ella, hold
your hand, imagine sixty years of marriage,
singing in the kitchen, *Come to mama,
come to mama do, my sweet embraceable you.*

9

A sweet embrace, mommy, is what we longed for
but never could manage until this forgetting.
I remember your pinches, swats called love slaps,
a warped tenderness. I pulled away from stiff
hugs, your cold child, hurt disguised as anger.
I vowed to hold my daughters as long
as they'd allow. And this is what we do now.
Who hurt you, I wonder, and why was touch
denied as if its tidal power would undo you?
Years of sharing a bed with our father,
yet no kissing in the kitchen, no cuddling
on the couch. We watched for signs of more
than habit, but the bedroom door stayed open
every night even after his poetry and flowers.

good close

His flowers, perennial, his poetry old fashioned,
he would say corny and nostalgic like the songs
in barbershop or in the car harmonizing
with you while we rolled our eyes and learned
the metaphors of another generation:
Over There, Blue Skies, The Old Rugged Cross.
On your birthdays he splurged with roses
and romantic cards, but it was after his own heart
wound down, after the close calls and bedside
visits, that he spoke love words out loud, even
wept and held tighter at hellos, goodbyes.
Like the beds of daisies and forget-me-nots
he came back each year to find
you'd grown further away.

11

You'd grown further away from the man
who vowed in his wedding poem to remain content
beside the deathless springs of your love, to weather
storms sure to sweep our quiet valley. We watched
him struggle to steer the ship, to remain calm
before the sure loss of his beloved. But he was taken
first and you didn't notice that he'd gone. In the hospital
with a feeding tube he wrote notes asking for you.
We drove you to his room, you touched his face,
said everything would be fine as if he'd never left.
His eyes knew this would be the last time, stricken
by love and cruel circumstance and you, left behind.
How to read his words sixty years later,
yesterday is a faded blur, tomorrow a happy haze.

Yesterday a faded blur, tomorrow a happy haze
leaves us with today, which is where you live now
in micro moments of peace or confusion, the Zen
master's lesson upended. I am trying, mother,
to live in this world, and it is bittersweet.
Did we find each other too late or just in time?
We have laid down our disappointments, disarmed
as two women who only need simple touch.
I can't remember, but there must have been a time
when you held me, when I gazed into your face
and felt an ease, an opening like grace. A time
before you became so large that I needed to push
away to prove that I was worthy. Your words
now gibberish, your voice always in my head.

Prayer to Asparagus

Your proud stalks

were never served

in my mother's kitchen.

Rich people's food.

Humble beans and carrots

until I found you standing

tall in Hadley dirt.

Come to me now, seared

and salted, mark me with

your weedy, primal odor.

Alchemy

There must be a hunger potion in this food,
says the child of my child as she eats
another plate of meatballs, a riff
on my Italian mother who charmed
my German father with a few peasant dishes
learned from her mother
who never finished school, but wearing
a sauce-stained apron spun out
pizzas dripping with mozzarella and salami,
savory rounds of locatelli-crusted bread,
and capeletti floating like lilies in broth.
No recipe in sight, my grandmother
kneaded and rolled out dough,
filled tiny pillows with meat, spinach,
and cheese, draped pale noodle strips over
the backs of chairs, while sauce bubbled
in a copper-bottomed cauldron for hours.

And though Mother vowed to be modern
with recipes clipped from ladies' magazines
to test on her pinochle crowd, the old dishes
bewitched us. Redolent of garlic, onions, marjoram,
basil sweating in butter, the brew simmered
on Saturday as we stood in line for confession,
our reward served after Sunday Mass.

When grandmother went blind from diabetes,
my mother policed all sweets until years later
her mind was irreversibly tangled.
She forgot the salt, collected twist-ties,

peppered the kitchen with yellow Post-its
scrawled with jumbled letters.
Like an intoxicated lover she
craved sugar, jammed the freezer
with Rocky Road and Vanilla Fudge,
stashed Snickers in drawers.
Lunch and dinner meaningless, she
served chocolate and caramel elixirs
until she was lost.

I imagine her at this table, set
with the pink-flowered plates I claimed
as great-grandchildren pronounce
the meatballs magical. And next to her
her mother's flour-dusted hands
gesture a sign for forgiveness,
Mangiamo.

Worker Man

My grandson's world blooms with yellow
trucks that dump, dig, lift and mix.
He wants to be a *worker man* and asks what
needs to be fixed with his tiny tools.
The adults pretend and wait for this play
to make way for serious tasks
like square roots. My grandfather

dropped out of school to raise his brothers
and sisters until the railroad took him.
After a strike, he and all the other strikers
were fired. He toted cement up ladders
to more skilled laborers until the work
wore him down. Then the crash and WPA
day jobs, long lines while his sons watched
trucks haul hungry men to sites
they'd never seen. I knew

him as janitor who walked to school
to stoke the boiler, empty trash, mop
floors before the children woke.
He brought me discarded workbooks,
a scratched desk. Unasked, he planted
flowers along sidewalks, more each year
until banks of iris, lilies and Shasta daisies
became the jewels of South Side's palette.

In a yellowed newspaper clipping
the principal shakes Bill's hand
for the gift of oasis in a grey city.
Bill would call it
a day's work, and work
with the right tools and clear purpose
is a revolution.

beautiful

This World

After rain in the woods, red newts
scramble from matted leaves and rotting
logs, beacon for a boy focused on
anything that moves. He scoops each
into a plastic bucket, counts twenty
wriggling bodies, notes distinguishing
traits -- white dot, fat legs, pale head.
By turns tender and rough, he holds
a favored one, reluctant to return
it to the wet dark, boundless
as anything he's felt. He will learn.
This world of wind creaks
and tree groans, fur and husk
will not be owned beyond
the lure of its wild singing.

A Five-Year-Old Creates Gender Theory

Buzz-cut plumber with diamond studs and Carharts

perplexes. *Are you a girl or a boy?*

Teen-aged cousin with long hair and soft voice

confuses. *Are you a girl or a boy?*

Two grandmothers kissing in the kitchen

amuses. *Do you love each other?*

Painted fingernails, dark shiny plums

spark a thrum deep inside that

refuses to be named.

Smalls

They spread across tables at flea markets,
spill out of boxes, mementos from a trip
or romance, collections of salt shakers,
heirloom silver spoons. After my parents die
I find a wax paper square with my name
and hank of fine flaxen hair, box of teeth
with rust-blood roots, hand-sewn dress.

My grandmother's hair is wrapped in tissue,
not the curled grey helmet I knew, but a long,
golden braid. Did she cut it off when her first
child was born, too worn out to care for
one more thing? It lies curled upon itself
like a soft animal, shimmering with lights
that must have lured her husband to unpin it
until the soft fall rained over his hands.

There are no silver cups, no engraved watches;
these smalls are stained bibs, hair and teeth
preserved like the relics my people prayed to
in the old country. Children were their saints,
the ones who would live larger, easier.

Now, my daughters are grown.
I pare down, save the chalk drawing
of a blue horse in the desert, the scent
that rose from my baby's skin,
a small blessing.

Underwear

Even a novocained heart
notices the hole
on the block
where your apartment
used to be, the room
where we first
kissed exploded to rubble,
and after, our house razed
to build an eco-friendly
fortress dark and empty.

Once a year we meet
for a litany
of trips, sick parents, dead pets.
Years flap, frayed
panties on the line
from which we
avert our eyes,
the delicate wreck
about which
we never speak.

Falling Asleep with Vin Scully

My father toted the kitchen transistor along with his
chores, sat through hours of games in the rec room with
his Phillies. Green vinyl recliner, Planter's peanuts,
Tom Sturgis pretzels and a Yuengling. Strike after
strike, base hits, extra innings, playoffs. I kept him
company although I could not crack the code of the
game, transfixed by his passion for cheers or curses,
this usually quiet man. And then I was bored and left
him to fall asleep alone.

Now my wife lies back in a Danish leather chair, sips
from a frosty mug for hours into the summer night.
Crickets and wood frogs riff along with Vin, the poet
laureate of baseball: *Pull up a chair, friends.* Strike after
strike, base hits, extra innings, playoffs. Vin paints each
Dodger nuance. In the next room, I drift away to the
amber flow of words, smooth as a scotch nightcap.
Forget it, there will always be another game.

Prayer to Salt

More than once your waves

tumbled me breathless,

spitting sand.

I used and used you

to blot blood stains,

to gargle and brine.

Threw you into stews

and over a shoulder

for savor or safety.

Licked tears and tried,

like Lot's wife

not to look back –

for too long.

Take my bones

and flesh, but please

preserve the sting

of memory.

About the Author

Gail Thomas, winner of the Charlotte Mew Prize of Headmistress Press, has published three books of poetry, *Waving Back, No Simple Wilderness: An Elegy for Swift River Valley,* and *Finding the Bear.*

Waving Back was named a Must Read for 2016 by the Massachusetts Center for the Book and received Honorary Mention by the New England Book Festival. Her work has appeared in many literary journals and anthologies including *The Beloit Poetry Journal, Calyx, Hanging Loose, The Chiron Review, Earth's Daughters, The North American Review,* and *Naugatuck River Review.* She is the recipient of grants from the Massachusetts Cultural Council and the Ludwig Vogelstein Foundation and was awarded residencies at the MacDowell Colony and Ucross.

Her book, *No Simple Wilderness,* about the drowning of towns and villages in Western Massachusetts in the 1930's to provide drinking water for Boston has been used as a text in college courses. As one of the original teaching artists for the state's Elder Arts Initiative, Gail collaborated with musicians, dancers, and storytellers across the state. She speaks at conferences and poetry festivals, reads her work widely in community and academic settings, and lives in Northampton, MA.

gailthomaspoet.com

Acknowledgments

My thanks to the editors of the following publications, in which these poems first appeared:

Naugatuck River Review: "Alchemy" (finalist, Narrative Poetry contest, Winter/Spring 2016)

Silkworm 9: "Worker Man"

Split Rock Review: "Smalls"

Valparaiso Poetry Review: "2" (published as "At the Van Gogh and Nature Exhibit")

Headmistress Press Books

The Great Scissor Hunt
Jessica K. Hylton

A Bracelet of Honeybees
Lynn Strongin

Whirlwind @ Lesbos
Risa Denenberg

The Body's Alphabet
Ann Tweedy

First name Barbie last name Doll
Maureen Bocka

Heaven to Me
Abe Louise Young

Tiger Laughs When You Push
Ruth Lehrer

Night Ringing
Laura Foley

Paper Cranes
Dinah Dietrich

A Crown of Violets
Renée Vivien tr. Samantha Pious

On Loving a Saudi Girl
Carina Yun

The Burn Poems
Lynn Strongin

31

I Carry My Mother
Lesléa Newman

Distant Music
Joan Annsfire

The Awful Suicidal Swans
Flower Conroy

Joy Street
Laura Foley

Chiaroscuro Kisses
G.L. Morrison

The Lillian Trilogy
Mary Meriam

Lavender Review
ed. Mary Meriam

Irresistible Sonnets
ed. Mary Meriam

Lady of the Moon
Amy Lowell
Lillian Faderman
Mary Meriam